50 Ways to Win New Customers

By
Paul R. Timm, Ph.D.

CAREER PRESS
180 Fifth Avenue
P.O. Box 34
Hawthorne, NJ 07507
1-800-CAREER-1
201-427-0229 (outside U.S.)
FAX: 201-427-2037

50 WAYS TO WIN NEW CUSTOMERS
ISBN 1-56414-072-5, $8.95
Cover design by Harvey Kraft
Printed by Book-mart Press

To order this title by mail, please include price as noted above, $2.50 handling per order, and $1.00 for each book ordered. Send to: Career Press, Inc., 180 Fifth Ave., P.O. Box 34, Hawthorne, NJ 07507

Or call toll-free 1-800-CAREER-1 (Canada: 201-427-0229) to order using VISA or MasterCard, or for further information on books from Career Press.

Library of Congress Cataloging-in-Publication Data

Timm, Paul R.
   50 ways to win new customers / by Paul R. Timm.
      p. cm.
   Includes index.
   ISBN 1-56414-072-5 : $8.95
   1. Small business--Management. 2. Advertising--Cost effectiveness. 3. Marketing--Cost effectiveness. 4. Customer service. I. Title. II. Title: Fifty ways to win new customers.
HD62.7.T5 1993
658.8--dc20
                                            93-7561
                                              CIP

Dedication

I am constantly amazed at the examples of symbolism over substance in organizations. Every organization talks about the importance of customers, and many have slogans touting that "the customer is number one" or "the customer is always right." But how many translate these slogans and good intentions into practical, day-to-day actions that win customers for life? Not many.

That's the good news! Because people and companies that get serious about winning customer—who create an ongoing strategy for doing so—will reap huge rewards.

This book, and my earlier Career Press book, *50 Powerful Ideas You Can Use to Keep Your Customers*, are my contributions to the cause of more satisfying customer relationships and more successful businesses.

As you read this book, make it your goal to identify five or six ideas for immediate application. Then look for several more you can use next month, and so forth. Make notes, scribble in the book. Try on new ideas and observe their results. By doing these things you will begin to harness the power of continuous quality improvement—and quantum leaps in your personal and organizational successes.

Remember the proverb: "God gives the birds their food, but he does not throw it into their nests."

This book is dedicated to those who recognize that there is no traffic on the extra mile—and to those who are determined to run it.

Contents

Introduction

Why businesses fail

1. Not enough customers   80%
2. Not the right customers   10%
3. Not the right products   10%

What's wrong with these pictures?

Jon and Marie Passive decided to start a business. They both loved reading, so a bookstore seemed like a natural. They contacted wholesalers, selected a product line they wanted to sell, and came up with a company name, *Verbose Books & Tapes*. They rented a store, put up an attractive sign, ran a few ads in the newspaper and sat back, expecting the customers to beat a path to their door for the best book and tape deals in town.

After a few months of sitting in their new store from 9 a.m. to 9 p.m., Jon and Marie realized that something just wasn't working quite the way they'd anticipated. They had very few customers.

Sandra and Ralph went a slightly different route in their search for business success. They bought a *Fat Freddy's* hamburger restaurant franchise ("home of the really big buns"). The home office gave them standardized training and lots of advice on how to make the restaurant profitable and keep costs down. But they didn't get much advice on how to compete with the *Wendel's Burger Hut* across the street. While Wendel's seemed to wallow in customers, Sandra's and Ralph's big buns went stale on the shelf.

Lynn's problem was a little different. Her variety store did really well for the first six years until a giant chain (*WallyWorld*) opened up nearby. *WallyWorld* was famous for selling a huge variety of goods at extremely competitive prices. It had been so successful at putting competitors under that the business press had dubbed them, "the merchant of death." How in the world can a small store like Lynn's compete with such a giant?

Finally we have Tom's situation. He works as a sales representative for a well-known office products company. His sales, especially in computer software, are off substantially. Most customers complain about a down market but he suspects they are buying elsewhere. Nobody wants to tell him directly, but they can get better service from his main competitor. And that's where they are going.

While these examples are from retailing, this basic problem arises in all kinds of businesses. In fact it is the single greatest business killer: the failure to *win* customers.

Not just get them to consider doing business with you, not just get them to buy once or twice, but to win them for the long run. That is the hallmark of any successful business or business person.

Apply the tips you'll learn in this book and you'll be light-years ahead of others in your ability to win customers. The process is simple, yet not easy. It can be applied in any organization or, for that matter, in any kind of relationship. The principles here can be used to strengthen marriages and families while also bolstering businesses. The techniques are the same. And your success will depend upon only four things:

- Awareness of the techniques available.
- Willingness to try some new ideas.
- Attention to the "little things."
- Consistent application.

In short, this book will show you how to double or triple your customer base and enjoy the highest possible profitability.

Pick your strategy

Before we look at specific techniques, let's consider a broader idea: your overall business strategy.

Business experts agree that in the 1990s, businesses must choose between one of two strategies. You can either be the high-quality, high-service leader (HQ/HS), or you can be the low-cost provider (LCP).

Either strategy can be successful but straddling the two is certain failure. Think about retailers again. The high-service department stores or specialty shops thrive year after year. (They may have downturns, of course, but over the long pull, they inevitably succeed so long as they stay with their HQ/HS strategy.) On the other hand, low-cost providers such as the no-frills warehouse stores and "I can get it for you wholesale" vendors also succeed as long as they stay with that LCP strategy.

The high-quality, high-service leader can command higher prices. Customers appreciate and are willing to pay more for HQ/HS. The successful low-cost provider makes it up in volume. However, and this is important, *to offer average quality products at average prices with average service...is the kiss of death.*

In many cases, the nature of your business rules out the LCP strategy. Health care and financial institutions, for example aren't likely to fare well as "Mayo Discount Clinic" or "Steve's Cut-Rate Financial Services."

Take a stand. Which do you want to be? HQ/HS or LCP? If HQ/HS is your choice, this book will be especially helpful to you. If LCP is your game, resell this book and get your money back. After all every penny counts when you're an LCP.

Where do customers come from?

The process of winning customers has several stages. First, we must get customers so that we can demonstrate our HQ/HS strategy to them. There are six ways to get customers:

1. **Attraction.** You win customers by projecting attitudes that cause customers to be interested in you and in your business.

2. **Conquest sales.** Here, the media trumpet your company's virtues so that people will remember you when they need what you sell. Even the customer who wanders into your life seemingly by accident was probably influenced by some form of advertising.

50 Ways to Win New Customers

3. **Invitation and incentives.** You draw the customer to you with special promotions, coupons, cold calling (phone or live) or referral follow-up.

4. **Retention of current customers.** This is the cheapest source of customers. They already know you and, if you treated them right, should feel some loyalty to you.

5. **Networking.** Your customers sell for you. Satisfied customers tell others about exceptional satisfaction—not as often as a dissatisfied one complains to others, but still they can become your best advertisers. Word-of-mouth advertising is still, and always will be, the most powerful form of marketing.

6. **Restoration of the "lost" customer.** Like the mythical Phoenix, customers can arise from the ashes. I'll show you how to resurrect them.

Part 1
Attraction

1.
Start with an attitude of gratitude.

Be thankful for customers. Customers are very special people. Of all the billions of people on this planet, only a tiny fraction will choose to do business with you. Treat your customers like the golden resources they are. Do you always do that?

If you or your employees have ever thought, "this would be such a great job if it weren't for the customers" you run a real risk of projecting that attitude. People have a sixth sense. If you see them as an inconvenience or burden, they'll sense it.

Nobody has to do business with you; they choose to. In making that choice, they are doing you a service. Sure, you provide them with important goods and services that meet their needs, but they still choose you. Be appreciative.

Also be appreciative that we live in a free country where we are free to compete for the approval of customers. Make the process of winning customers a lifelong hobby; make it fun.

Commit, starting today, to love your customers.

2.
Don't try to teach a pig to dance.

If you don't have that attitude of gratitude, or if you simply don't like people, throw this book away. You'll never win or keep customers. It's OK. Don't feel bad. Just accept yourself for what you are and go into a job that doesn't require contact with others (if you can find one).

Likewise, when you hire employees, be sure they like people. Watch the ways they interact with all kinds of people. Be sure you are careful in selecting who will represent your company. Don't take the hiring process lightly or grab the most convenient available person (like a relative or friend of a friend).

Anyone can fake behaviors for a while, but if you observe your prospective employees carefully, you'll see how well they hold their positive attitude. They'll probably work for you for a long time, so be sure you hire right in the first place.

I recall interviewing for a job as a sales representative for Xerox years ago. Each time I thought they had decided to hire me, I learned that someone else wanted to do another interview. This went on for weeks and I was eager to get on with the job. Frankly, I was getting frustrated and was tempted to tell them to fish or cut bait. I needed a decision.

Now I see what they were doing. They were testing my frustration level. They wanted to see how I'd act when a customer would waffle on a buying decision.

3.
Do an organizational reality check.

Most companies say that the customer is number one. Sure, sure. But before you start believing your own press clippings (or advertisements), come up with answers to these *potentially disquieting questions about customer service in your organization* that I ask my clients:

Does your company...

1. Talk about customer service but pay front-line people a low, flat wage?

2. Offer little or no ongoing training in the basics of good service for customer contact people?

3. Offer no special incentives for taking care of the customer?

4. Punish or reprimand an employee's poor customer service but take good service for granted?

5. Place greater emphasis on winning new customers than retaining ones you already have?

6. Offer no awards or recognition for employees who support contact people's efforts to serve customers?

7. Hold "be nice to the customer" programs or campaigns that last for a few weeks or months but are soon forgotten?

8. Have top managers who rarely, if ever, face live customers or devote time to listening to customers and helping them solve problems?

9. Make no effort to measure service quality as perceived by customers?

10. Make no attempt to hold managers at all levels accountable for the service level?

An affirmative answer to any of these questions can be a red flag to you. While all organizations talk about customer satisfaction, many unwittingly discourage it by doing the things described above. Where does your organization stand?

4.
Judge not,
assume the best.

Joe Girard (who modestly bills himself as "the world's greatest salesman") talks about the importance of having a positive attitude toward all people. Don't judge them or put them into some category. Assume they are and will continue to be your customer. Joe puts it this way:

> "However I feel about myself or whoever I'm with, I don't let my feelings get in the way. This [selling] is a business we're in, an important profession. And those people, those prospects, those customers are the most important thing in the world to us, to each of us. They aren't interruptions or pains in the ass. They are what we live on. And if we don't realize that, as a hard business fact, then we don't know what we are doing. I'm not talking about some of them or most of them. I'm talking about all of them."[1]

Sales trainers teach people to be "assumptive." *Assume* that a person is going to buy, and treat him or her accordingly. The power of the assumptive really works. It's like positive thinking. It somehow projects to the customer and becomes a self-fulfilling prophecy.

---

[1] Joe Girard, *How to Sell Anything to Anybody* (New York: Simon and Schuster, 1977), p. 47.

J. D. Salinger said, "I am a kind of paranoid in reverse. I suspect people of plotting to make me happy." With an attitude like that, we'd look forward to every meeting with every customer.

Of course, we quickly learn that some customers do *not* seem to be plotting to make us happy. Most are very pleasant. Some are unusual. A few are downright difficult. Occasionally you face the Customer from Hell.

Every person is different; each has a unique personality. But the kind of people who tend to bug us the most are the ones who are *not like us.* Accept this diversity and learn to enjoy it. Know that people's needs are basically the same at some level and that *treating them like guests* will create the most goodwill and a powerful basis for good customer relations.

5.
Look in the mirror.

From the moment we meet people, we begin to size them up. What we decide about their trustworthiness and ability is largely a factor of first impressions. And, as the old saying goes, you only get one chance to make that first impression.

An owner of an auto repair shop tried an experiment. He paid each of his repair people on commission for the amount of repair work they did. He invited the mechanics to volunteer to change their dress and grooming. Several agreed to cut their hair, shave daily and wear clean uniforms. Those who did, created far more repeat business than the others. The customers would ask for the better dressed mechanics and those who chose to dress and groom themselves in the "old way" found they were getting less work.

The key word in dress and grooming is *appropriate*. Sales people in a surf shop would look foolish in three-piece suits; an undertaker would look ludicrous in a Hawaiian sport shirt.

The importance of dress explains why some organizations provide uniforms. It used to be more widespread. Nurses, delivery people and bank employees were given attractive full or partial uniforms that projected professionalism. Many employees appreciated this. It saved them money on a work wardrobe. Perhaps it's time for a revival of such a practice. It would certainly set an organization apart from its competition.

6.
Check the appearance of your work area.

"A cluttered desk is the sign of a cluttered mind," says the desk plaque. Likewise, a cluttered business or work area conveys a sense of disorganization and low professionalism.

Look around you and see what your customer sees. Is merchandise displayed attractively? Is the place clean and tidy? Does the work space look organized and efficient?

Granted, some people work very well in a mass of clutter. I know of a plumbing supply store that looks like a tornado casualty, yet the old-timer who runs the place can find anything he needs. I also know more then a few professors who seem to thrive amongst an avalanche of paper. But these are rare birds.

If you find yourself spending too much work time looking for things or helping customers find misplaced items, it's time to de-junk.

7.
Be an explorer.

When you hear about a great idea another business is using, send out an exploration party to scope it out.

One supermarket known for exceptional service encourages employees to take a company van and rush to the scene of good service given by others. They take notes and discuss possible implementation in their store.

Other explorer groups can be customers or employees who report their findings to management. Be open to these ideas. Keep your eyes and ears open for new ideas. Sometimes they come from the most unlikely sources.

Part 2
Conquest sales

8.
Broadcast your successes.

Let people know how you help customers. Let people know about situations when you have helped customers identify applications for your products that may be unusual.

Use the business press. Columnists for local newspapers are constantly looking for new material. If you have an interesting story to tell, contact them. A phone call will usually tell you whether you have something they'd be interested in.

Journalists need stories, and if you have a story or a new product, service or application, they will be interested.

If you are uncomfortable with a cold phone call, write a press release and then follow up with a call.

If you aren't good at writing or don't have the time, contact a nearby university's journalism or communication department. Ask if there are students who would like some "real-world" experience in writing press releases. Many students will jump at the opportunity. Pay them a few dollars for any releases that make the news.

Broadcasting doesn't have to involve the mass media. Post a bulletin board with photos of new customers (pictured with your product) and letters that compliment your company. If a particularly good letter comes in, call the writer and ask if it could be used in your advertising. Then run an ad showing the letter.

9.
Be a good citizen.

Be a corporate good citizen and your efforts will be rewarded. Indirect advertising via sponsorship of community events is a good way to plant the name of your company in the minds of potential customers.

Jack, a good friend of mine, has a clear set of corporate values. He is dedicated to producing and distributing high-quality products at modest cost while giving back a portion of his profits back to his community.

Jack has chosen a local charity that he feels strongly about—the Easter Seals Foundation—and he looks for opportunities to help them. At Christmas time he sends his customers, suppliers and other business associates a letter wishing them a happy holiday season and indicating that he has made a contribution to the Easter Seals Foundation in their name. A few days later, these same people get a letter from the charity acknowledging the gift Jack made in their name. A double reminder of Jack's goodwill!

10.
Stay current with new business ideas or applications.

Read the business press and keep your eyes open for new ideas. For example, one very hot topic as I write this, is indoor air quality. A business that offers janitorial services should probably consider expanding into "interior environment" services. One logical expansion is to offer to pressure vacuum heating and air-conditioning vents to remove buildup of dust, pollens, fungi, etc.

I never knew such businesses existed until I saw a business column write-up describing the health problems and allergies associated with indoor air quality.

Adding a new service or product line provides a great reason to contact your existing customers, too. Let them know what's new via phone, letter or media ads.

11.
Take advantage of new communication technology.

There have never been more ways to advertise, promote and market products.

A few simple examples: Many organizations rely widely on the use of fax machines to receive and send messages. Deli restaurants receive lunchtime orders for delivery via fax. Companies respond to customer requests for information via fax.

Another new technology is the 900 phone lines. In the past these were associated with "telephone sex" or porno lines. This has changed (in fact, sexually explicit talk is prohibited on 900 lines). As the stigma of 900 lines is reduced, their use for disseminating information will be more widespread. Such lines can be established with recorded messages or live operators. The 900 services bill the caller for the call and typically provide some specialized information. These can be coupled with fax communication to automatically send a print message back to the caller.

Computer networks and electronic bulletin boards can match people's needs with products and services available. Check computer periodicals for more ideas and applications.

12.
Get to know your "A" customers.

The ever-popular 80/20 Rule—80 percent of your business will come from 20 percent of your customers—really does have validity. (Also, 80 percent of your profits will come from 20 percent of your products, but that's another story.) Get to know those crucial 20 percenters that account for most of your success.

Ironically, some businesses don't have much respect for their "A" customers. Banking executives, for example, sometimes look upon people with high debt with some disdain, yet people who owe banks money are their best customers. Candy shop or toy store owners who get irritated with kids may be griping about their best customers. And retailers who prejudge a customer's ability to buy are often dumbfounded when someone not matching their "profile" turns out to be a legitimate "A" customer.

I recently talked with a man who had a $4 million line of credit at a local bank. This fellow was not known for sartorial splendor (he dressed like a slob). When he asked a teller for some crisp $10 bills to give his grandchildren, she gave him a hard time. He was patient, but when she refused to stamp his parking ticket, he went to a nearby officer and inquired about the possibility of withdrawing his funds.

When the officer saw who it was, some serious tap dancing took place and the account was saved. But the teller wasn't. She became a casualty of ignorance and poor service compounded by being unaware of an "A" customer.

13.
Give more than just a business card.

Swapping business cards has become a cliché, and, like a cliché, it often goes unnoticed. Here are some ways to boost the effect of giving a card:

1. Have your card designed to include your photo.

2. Print a saying or quote on the back—something customers will enjoy and remember. (I know one fellow who had a cartoon about his profession on the back of his card.)

3. Write a personalized note on it.

4. Write your home phone on it, implying to the receiver an interest in being friends or of your willingness to serve in any way possible.

5. Staple a brochure or sample to the card. Maybe even a flower.

6. Clip your card to a newspaper or magazine article of interest to the recipient.

7. Give cards freely. One company directed that every piece of first-class mail sent out include a business card—even the bills they paid! This led to a call from the local electric company asking about their products. Another fellow literally tossed his cards in the air at football games when

the home team scored. Cards do no good sitting in your desk drawer. Get them out.

8. Display your card prominently on your desk, counter or with sales literature. Encourage people to take one—or a handful of them—if they might know other interested customers.

9. Offer a bonus to people who refer your card to friends. Have them write their name on the back and when a prospect comes in showing the card, reward the person who gave it to him.

Let creativity be your guide. I read about a woman who wanted to expand her accounting practice, so she bought a small ad in her local newspaper. She had the printer leave the ad blank except for a line across the bottom asking readers to file her business card for future reference. As the papers came off the press, she and her husband stuck her photo business card into the blank space with double-stick tape. Months later she was still hearing from readers.[2]

Do not try this with *The New York Times*, of course.

---

[2] This and lots of other good ideas are found in *Guerrilla Selling*, by Bill Gallagher, Orvil Ray Wilson and Jay Conrad Levinson (Houghton Mifflin, 1993), p. 40.

14.
Project an image in advertising.

Advertising materials get much more bang for the buck if they look somewhat alike. Use the same company logo, slogans, colors and themes. Changing these too often confuses the customer.

Keep your advertising theme simple. Select slogans or mottoes that clearly and simply state what your company stands for. The fewer words, the better.

Look at the advertising giants. Coke, Pepsi, Proctor & Gamble, auto manufacturers, TV networks, etc. They always have simple, short ad slogans. Likewise the giant retailers who use "Satisfaction guaranteed" or "Where America Shops" to convey a simple message. One of my favorites is from Land's End, the direct merchant clothing giant. It's motto is, "Guaranteed. Period." That's it. Two words that say a mouthful.

If you don't have an ad slogan or organizational theme, get your people together and come up with one.[3]

---

[3] See Paul R. Timm, *50 Powerful Ideas You Can Use to Keep Your Customers* (Career Press, 1992), pp. 46-50. See page 91 of this book to order.

15.
Showroom/showcase your products or services.

Even if your business doesn't sell a tangible product, find something tangible that you can display. Even if you sell only by phone, direct mail or through distributors, have a display of your products neatly arranged in the public part of your office.

Explore the possibility of displaying at the airport or bus station where people often have time to kill. A display case with tool sets, artwork for sale and executive planners have caught my interest in airports.

Maybe you can get a complimentary business to allow you to display your stuff in their place. For example, a small home furnishings display might work well in a real estate office. Or a showcase for your health spa or sporting goods could be interesting to patrons in a beauty salon.

16.
Check out trade shows, fairs and flea markets.

As with anything, there are tricks to this trade show business. A lot of people think they can just set up a table with a display and customers will flock to them. Sorry, it's not that simple.

Here are some tips from the pros:

1. **Pre-invite potential customers to visit your booth.** Get lists of convention attendees in advance, if possible. Send them a letter of invitation and a card they can redeem at your booth for a prize or gift. When I was president of a training company, we told convention attendees that if they brought the letter we sent them to our booth and viewed our seven-minute introductory video, they'd receive a free calculator. When the expo opened, people came running!

2. **Make your giveaway prominent.** Example: A computer software producer selling a tape backup system (so you wouldn't lose stored data) gave away a kid's bank shaped like a safe. This six-inch cube was pretty bulky to carry around the expo, but people who saw others with it asked how they could get one too. The prize attracted attention and tied in with the company's product theme.

3. **Work the booth!** Instruct all employees working at the booth that this is not a passive venture. Don't sit down. Greet all guests. Pre-plan an opening gambit to create interest.

4. **Follow up all leads.** Quickly contact any leads you get from the booth. The key word here is *quickly*. Prospect leads get cold very fast.

17.
Publish a book.

A friend of mine published a paperback book called *How to Avoid Auto Service Ripoffs.* Guess what business he is in?

His book bore a $7.95 price tag but was either sold at a deep discount in his shop or given away. The book had many tips, but its more important function was that it told customers that they wouldn't be ripped off at *his* business.

People trust what they see in print. A publication projects credibility and trust.

Isn't writing a book a lot of work? Sure. But there are people who can help you. Check with a university's journalism or public relations program to see if there are students with good writing skills who would like a chance to become a published author. After you've seen samples of the student's writing, negotiate a flat fee (typically a few hundred dollars will do it) and tell the writer that he or she will be listed as a co-author.

Then sit down with your tape recorder and spill your guts. Give the tapes to the ghost writer and watch their youthful enthusiasm have at it.

18.
Teach prospective customers.

An auto repair shop offers a series of seminars on how cars work. These sessions are free and the public is invited. Each week, people can choose the mini-course they'd like to attend. A mechanic explains brakes, suspension systems, mufflers and pollution controls, and other aspects of how cars work. After the classes, people are invited for coffee and donuts.

This service helps potential customers feel comfortable around the business and gets them acquainted with the employees.

Other business people volunteer to come into schools, church groups or civic organizations to teach about their products or services. Craft stores, survival gear, home storage products, cosmetics, home cleaning solutions, etc., have been effectively publicized through free demonstrations or classes. How about your products?

19.
List your business in phone directories.

Yellow pages are a must for any business that deals with the general public. You need not have the largest ad, but you do need to be listed. Likewise, take advantage of listing opportunities in professional directories or memberships.

Better still, use the directories available to locate customers. A trip to your local business library will be time well spent. Learn what kinds of directories are available. If you sell to other businesses, books like the Dun & Bradstreet *Million Dollar Directory* or *MacRae's Blue Book* will give you basic information about every business in a particular region. Generally you can get the names of key people (including purchasing agents), branch and home office locations, and even their credit ratings. You can then contact the companies about your products, or better yet gather information about them that may give you tips on how to meet their needs.

Another directory used by savvy business people is *R. L. Polk City Directory* found at the library's reference desk. This book lists every household (denoting home owners) and business by address and lots of additional information. New home owners and businesses are also noted.

Finally, while you are at the library, review trade journals that target your industry. Look for feature articles that show what successful people are doing.

Read with the intent of gathering new ideas or applications you can use.

20.
Cross-promote with another business.

Tire dealer Les Schwab built his highly successful business in the Pacific Northwest. In the early 1960s, Les hatched an idea with the Oregon Cattlemen's Association to give beef certificates to tire buyers. In his autobiography, he describes his "free beef" promotion.

> *"It has been one of our most successful promotions in that it helps to promote the sale of beef, and also the sale of tires. From almost the first day of my business I had made up my mind that I wanted the business of the rancher. I can safely say that ranchers have been the backbone of my business for 34 years. I have specialized in ranch tires from car tires, pickup tires, truck, tractor and oddball sizes to fit various ranch equipment."*[4]

Tire buyers received a $7.50 to $15 certificate toward the purchase of beef, depending on how many tires they bought. Most customers bought even more beef than the free certificate allowed. Les cross-promoted by:

1. Identifying a key group of customers (ranchers).
2. Finding a way to promote their interests.
3. Creating a feeling of partnership.

---

[4] Les Schwab, *Les Schwab Pride in Performance* (Bend, Oregon: Maverick Publishers, 1986), p. 47.

21.
Train your people well.

Ultimately a company's employees are its best advertisers. Be sure all employees have ample training. The most frequent mistake companies make in seeking short-term savings is to cut training.

Japanese companies often put their people through much more training than we do. I've been told of department store elevator operators who are trained for months so that they know a great deal about people and the store. They can tell you where to find virtually anything in the place.

Obviously, training need not always be in a classroom setting although some should be. Assigning more experienced employees to newer ones can create a mentoring relationship as the old hand teaches the rookie what to do. (Be sure the mentor has the best work skills and habits.)

An often overlooked benefit of ongoing training is that it is appreciated by employees. They feel good when their company spends time and money to make them more professional.

22.
Rebuild a weak reputation.

Suppose you do an organizational reality check (#3 earlier), looking at your company through your customer's eyes, and you don't much like what you see. What now?

Face the situation directly and let people know you are committed to rebuilding your ability to serve customers well. K-Mart, the second-largest retailer in the world, has recently dedicated more than $3 billion of its budget to store revitalization, largely in response to the competitive threat of Wal-Mart (now the world's largest retailer).

Here's an example on a smaller scale: The owner of a tire store chain used old-fashioned sincerity to invite customers back to his store. He sent an open letter to his community that apologized for poor service they might have experienced in the past. Here is his letter (modified slightly to protect the guilty):

ReallyBig Tire Stores
Auto Service Centers
123 Main
Bison Breath, Nebraska

Oct. 1, 1996

An Open Letter to the People of Bison Breath

Some time ago, we discovered that our previous manager and his staff were not taking care of our customers at our Bison Breath store. This is certainly not in keeping with ReallyBig Tire's guarantee of customer satisfaction, qualified technicians and friendly service. We were extremely disappointed to hear this and we tried to move quickly to correct the situation.

The previous manager was discharged, and on June 27 we transferred Craig Cunningham into the Bison Breath store. Craig is a very competent, courteous manager with years of experience in the tire and automotive industry. Craig, his wife and family are long-term residents of nearby Eastville. Since Craig has been your store manager, we have had many positive comments on his service and dedication to customers' needs.

To show our good faith, and to welcome folks back to our store at 123 Main, we will perform a full lubrication service; change the oil with up to five quarts of Pennzoil oil, install a new oil filter and lube the chassis for only $5.95 upon presentation of this letter at the store.

We are happy to be part of the growing Bison Breath community and will do our best to offer tires and automotive services at the lowest prices in Nebraska with the finest service anywhere.

Sincerely,

James Williams

cc: Honorable James Williams, Mayor
    City of Bison Breath

23.
Show that you honor customer satisfaction.

A radio station in Florida created a promotion honoring people who give good service. WLKF in Lakeland invites listeners to write to them about great service they witness. Listeners are encouraged to describe the service excellence they see, the name of the company and the name of the person who gave the great service. People cited have their name put into a drawing for a cruise vacation.

I suggested a similar promotion to one of my clients in another part of the country. They contacted a local radio station and arranged to jointly sponsor the contest. The station provided air time while the client's organization funded the vacation prize. The spot on the radio went something like this:

"WXXX and Moose Lips Outdoor Stores recognize the importance of good customer service. Better service builds a stronger economic climate throughout Whitebread County. So here's your chance to reward someone who went the extra mile to give you great service.

Send or fax your description of service excellence you've received to WXXX. Be sure to include the name of the business, the date and time of your experience, and the name of the employee who helped you. Nominated employees will qualify for an all-expense paid cruise on the Mexican Riviera to be given away on March 13.

Join WXXX and Moose Lips Outdoor Stores in celebrating great service!"

This joint campaign links your organization with the concept of service excellence. While appearing to be almost a public service, your company gets positioned as one with a high concern for excellent customer satisfaction.

24.
Donate to a charity.

Researchers have found that they can significantly increase the likelihood that people will respond to a survey when they offer a donation to charity for each returned survey. Even compared against surveyors who enclose 50 cents or a dollar as a token of appreciation, the charity approach works better. The cash reward is too small to be meaningful to recipients but they feel good about the charity donation.

A similar approach can be used to get new customers to look at your company. Offer a donation for a test drive or demonstration of your product. Better yet, give your customers a choice of three different charities.

Part 3
Invitation and incentives

25.
Use coupon books or punch cards for repeat customers.

A few months ago, a woman came to my door selling a coupon booklet for a local dry cleaner. The booklet offered some $200 worth of discounts and cost $35. She offered to sell it to me for just $29. I checked her references (which she cheerfully provided) and realized that the dry cleaner was one I occasionally used. So I bought.

Then I asked how this promotion worked. She explained that she got to keep a substantial part of the $29 and that the cleaner absorbed the remaining discounts by increasing customer traffic. A win-win situation.

An auto repair shop used a similar approach with a twist. It printed up coupon books and donated them to the local high school. High school kids then sold the booklets and kept the proceeds. The repair business built traffic and increased its customer base. Its costs in the short term were more than made up for in repeat customers.

Be sure your business is ready to handle increased customer loads and, by all means, be sure all employees are informed about the promotion. Nothing kills the benefits of such an effort faster than having a clerk who responds, "I can't accept those coupons."

26.
Consider a door-to-door approach.

Door-to-door sales can work well, especially if your customers don't expect to be reached in this way.

Try canvassing homes or businesses nearby. Use an informational, friendly approach, not a hard sell. Simply let people know that you are in the neighborhood and would appreciate their business.

If people are not home or prefer not to talk, just leave a flier or brochure.

So few people do door-to-door business anymore that it creates an element of surprise. Be sure to be sensitive to privacy, and avoid canvassing at times when people might consider your appearance an interruption. Keep it low-key and non-threatening.

27.
Try a letter campaign.

A variation on phone or door-to-door prospecting is a letter campaign. For almost every business, there are people out there who would be happy to buy from you *if they only knew you were available to them.*

I often think about the process of buying an automobile. For most of us it's a rather unpleasant task. Cars cost a lot of money and we want to feel certain that we are getting a good value. We feel best about this when we are buying from someone we trust and like—when we buy from a friend.

Don't you wish you had a trusted friend in the car business? For most of us, we never will have such a friend unless we go to the dealer and make a friend. Initiating such a friendship is uncomfortable for most people.

The alert car salesperson sees the opportunity to get new customers by building friendships. Such people are active in community, church, civic or volunteer groups and aren't bashful about letting people know that they sell cars.

You don't have to be an aggressive, high-pressure salesperson to make such contacts in your community. In fact, your approach should be exactly the opposite. Make friends first, then make it easy for your friends to do business with you.

A friendly letter like this one on the may work wonders:

Dear Betty:

Just a note to tell you how much I enjoy working with you in the Soup Kitchen (or Rotary Club, or Church Youth Program or whatever). I value your friendship and feel good about what we have been able to accomplish.

If I can ever be of help to you in purchasing a car (or insurance or computer or business services or whatever you sell), please give me a call.

Again, thanks for your friendship. See you next Tuesday.

Regards,

Tom

Tom

Would people be insulted or offended by such a note? Very rarely. It's low-key and expresses appreciation for the reader while simply reminding individuals that you would welcome them as customers.

Remember the undertaker's motto: "Everybody will be a customer someday. Make friends and they'll be *your* customer."

28.
Build and maintain a prospect list.

This isn't just for insurance salespeople. Try it.

Make a list including everyone you can think of who might need your products or services. Don't be too selective. Think about every situation where you come across different people. List friends, business associates, members of organizations you belong to, old school friends, people you buy products and services from, and more.

Whether you use a computer or a large legal pad, put one name on each line. If you have phone numbers and addresses, fine. But get the name down even if you'll need to look up additional information in order to contact the person.

Look at your list regularly, anytime you have a break in business, from the customers you are serving. Add to the list often as new people come to mind.

Once people on the list become real prospects (they have a need or have indicated some interest) "promote" them to your card file or to a prospect file on your computer. Then use *this* file for follow-up.

Don't just wait for people to wander into your place of business. Contact *them*. Make it a habit to reach out to potential customers every day.

I knew a young man I'll call Tom, who came out of the military service and decided that he wanted to run his own business. He had no experience and wasn't even sure what he'd do. He just knew that he wanted to be his own boss.

For his first venture, Tom worked a deal with a wholesaler of small appliances. Tom could get good-quality products at very attractive prices. He set up a small store and, at first, did what almost every other store owner does: He ran a few newspaper ads and waited for customers to come in and buy.

Guess what? They didn't.

Tom was an impatient sort. A take-charge guy. So, instead of sitting around waiting, he created a list of people he knew and began calling them. His pitch to them was low-key. He simply told the truth: He had started a new business and it was going pretty slow. He wondered if they knew of anyone who might have a need for a small appliance.

In other words, he just asked for the business.

Wow! What a revolutionary idea! Of course it isn't. It's common sense, yet how many small store owners do you know who do this?

Tom's story has a happy ending as you might guess. He succeeded in his first store and went on to develop a chain of appliance stores that have earned him a handsome living.

Part 4
Retention of current customers

29.
E-Plus: The master key to customer satisfaction.

There is no more powerful way to win repeat customers than to *exceed* their expectations. E-Plus is the term I use to remind people of this process:

1. Constantly strive to sharpen your understanding of what customers want from you. Be specific and objective.

2. Consistently seek ideas for exceeding these expectations.

Let me put on my psychologist's hat for a moment here and explain why E-Plus is so powerful.

Customers are rational people. If a buying experience is positive, they might come back; if negative, they'll try to avoid returning. The challenge is to improve the probability that they will come back. But customers who are satisfied may be *inert*, not motivated. Their satisfaction simply means the *absence of dissatisfaction*, not the motivation to become a repeat customer. A zone of indifference exists between the dissatisfied and the motivated. The challenge, then, is to get beyond satisfaction to motivation.

The crucial role of customer expectations

Customers entering into a transaction, bring a range of expectations (albeit perhaps unconsciously) about what the transaction will be like. What they expect is based on past experience with your business or ones like it. These mental expectations are *perceptual*. They exist in the mind of the customer. Sometimes they are accurate and rational; sometimes they aren't. Perceptions of customer satisfaction go beyond just the quality of the core product or service. They take into account the whole buying experience. Expectations will vary among different organizations or under differing circumstances. For example, people expect different treatment from a full-service retailer than they do from a warehouse store. They won't expect the same service from a prestigious law firm and a state auto license bureau.

Different expectations from different businesses

Suppose you intend to shop at a low-cost, self-service, discount store. Going into the store, you anticipate a certain kind of experience. You do not necessarily expect that the clerk (if you can find one) in the clothing department will be an expert in fitting clothing. Nor would you expect that person to be particularly helpful in coordinating items you may want to purchase. This is not to say that some people who work there would not have these skills, but you probably wouldn't expect this as a general rule.

If you simply select some clothing items from a rack and take them to a checkout for purchase, you are not surprised nor particularly disappointed. That is about what you expected, and if other aspects of the store are satisfactory (it seems clean and well-stocked, for instance) you could be perfectly satisfied.

By contrast, if you go to a high-quality, high-service clothing store or a boutique, you expect a different kind of transaction. You probably expect to be served by people who have expertise in clothing fit, color and materials. You might realistically expect personal attention and assistance as you make your purchases.

One of three situations—negative, neutral or positive—will result as customers compare their expectations with the service received:

Negative	Neutral	Positive
• Positive expectations failed. • Negative expectations confirmed.	• Expectations met.	• Negative expectations failed. • Positive or neutral expectations exceeded.

In the situation described in the left column, the customer's experience was worse than expected. She's dissatisfied and likely to defect to another provider, if she has a rational alternative. The middle-column customer is neither dissatisfied nor particularly motivated to return. This is the zone of indifference.

In the right-column situation, the transaction was better than expected. Either the customer thought it would be pretty good—and it was *very* good, or the customer thought it would not be very good but it wasn't as bad as expected. If positive expectations were sufficiently exceeded (or negative ones shown to be unfounded), this customer is a good candidate for repeat business. The right-column situation is an E-Plus experience—customer expectations were *exceeded*.

Why E-Plus leads to customer retention

A social psychological theory called Equity Theory explains why we can predict that the E-Plus (right-column) customer will become a repeat customer.

Equity Theory considers all kinds of social relationships ranging from the intimate to the cursory. The buyer-seller situation is one such relationship.

In any relationship, people constantly assess the relative *equity* of their involvement compared to other relationships. They regularly check to see if what they give to the relationship balances with what they get out of it.

The theory predicts what people will do when they perceive inequity. When the person thinks the business is getting the better deal in this relationship, the customer will respond with one or some combination of the following:

- **Ignore or rationalize the inequity.** The customer concludes that the service is poor but it's poor everywhere. The world isn't fair but it's not worth fighting it.

- **Demand restitution.** The offended person demands fairer treatment, or the customer wants his money back.

- **Retaliation.** The offended person speaks badly of the organization or person seen as the cause of the inequity. Outright sabotage is an extreme form of retaliation.

- **Withdraw from the relationship.** The customer refuses to do further business with the organization or person.

Hence, the dissatisfied customer is likely to do one of these things. The first two alternatives may give a business a chance to patch things up and retain the customer. But the last two can be devastating.

Customers often retaliate for perceived inequity by telling other people about poor service received. The typical unhappy customer tells 10 to 20 others about his or her experience, studies say. These negative ripple effects can result in scores or even hundreds of lost customers or potential customers.

But there is another side to Equity Theory that predicts this: People who feel that they are receiving more than they *deserve* from a transaction also experience a psychological need to restore balance. A simple example is the social pressure you might feel to reciprocate after being invited to someone's home for dinner. The relationship will remain unbalanced until you equalize it with a similar kindness.

Herein lies the theoretical basis for exceeding customer expectations. By going beyond the expected, you create an imbalance that, for many people, requires action on their part to rebalance. They may rationalize or ignore it, of course. But attempts to restore the balance can also take the form of:

- Telling others of the positive experience.

- Paying a premium for the goods received.

- Becoming a repeat customer.

The challenge, then, is to *create positive imbalances by exceeding customer expectations*. This is E-Plus.

Explain E-Plus to all employees. Then schedule regular brainstorming sessions where everyone can have fun coming up with new E-Plus ideas.

30.
E-Plus with added value.

When I ask people to describe value that exceeds their expectations, I hear tales of exceptional products like 15-year-old Kirby vacuum cleaners and 20-year-old Western Auto freezers. Often people talk about their Ford or Toyota pickup truck with 200,000 miles on it, or a sweater that dates back a quarter century. These products exceeded the customers' expectations of value. They got more than they expected for their money.

Value is determined by the quality of the product or service compared to its price. Sometimes something as simple as packaging can enhance the perceived value. Stores that gift-wrap goods or provide customers with high-quality shopping bags can project additional value.

A department store where I shop always gives me a vinyl, zip-up hanger bag when I buy a suit or sportcoat. Some bookstores and gift shops have attractive and sophisticated wrapping paper for goods sold. These can create E-Plus in customer's minds.

Keep in mind that E-Plus has two sides to it: the expected and the received. Be sure your customers have realistic expectations about your products. If they unrealistically expect something to last 10 years and it's only designed to last five, be sure to clarify that.

How can *your* business give more value than expected?

31.
E-Plus with added information.

My son recently had knee surgery. The therapist not only explained what exercises he should do but also gave him photocopied sheets illustrating exactly how do them. She wrote his name at the top of each sheet and numbered the sequence.

Enlightened auto salespeople spend time with the customer—after the sale—explaining all the features on the new car. A hospital client changed the signs and installed color stripes on the corridor floors to direct people to various departments. A cellular phone dealer calls customers to see if they understand how to use their phone's features and offers to meet to explain them in person.

E-Plus often means providing information in a more usable or personalized form. Companies might provide instructional videos, hands-on lessons, or step-by-step checklists. Many have gone to 800 numbers for customer assistance or advice. Some provide users newsletters or new application ideas for their product.

How can *your* business give customers more useful information?

32.
E-Plus with better speed.

A well-known air freight company claims to deliver packages by 10 a.m. the next morning, but they often arrive by 9 or 9:30. The repair office for a major office equipment company makes it a point to have the service person arrive earlier than promised.

At a supermarket, additional cashiers open when more than two customers are in line. Some fast-food restaurants have your lunch up almost before you can order it.

Incidentally, my research into customer "pet peeves" has shown clearly that the number-one turnoff is slow or inefficient service. Even restaurants where you might expect leisurely dining to be the expectation were downgraded in the mind of customers if the service was perceived as too slow.[5]

Are there ways you can give the customer faster service than he or she expects?

---

[5] For a condensed report of research findings, see Paul R. Timm and Kristen DeTienne, *From Slogans to Strategy: A Workable Approach to Customer Satisfaction and Loyalty* in EXCHANGE (a publication of the Marriott School of Management, Brigham Young University), Spring 1993.

33.
E-Plus with better price.

A repair shop with E-Plus in mind tells a customer the job will cost "about $200" and then comes in at $194.50. The customer is astonished. It actually costs *less* than expected! (Note that if the price comes in at $205.50, you've lost the E-Plus. The amount isn't as important as the fact that it went over estimate.) This shop intentionally quotes a figure slightly higher that what the final cost will be. It runs a risk of possibly losing a customer to a lower bid, but once customers experience E-Plus, they'll come back regularly and tell others about the good deal they got.

Keep in mind that price is not always a major determinant of satisfaction. Remember our discussion of high-quality, high-service compared to low-cost providers? If you are positioned for an HQ/HS strategy, price will be far less of an issue in the customer's mind.

Nevertheless, customers always appreciate a price that turns out a bit more attractive than expected. If the value is there, the price will not pose a barrier to customer satisfaction.

How can *your* organization exceed pricing expectations?

34.
E-Plus with add-ons.

A shoe store clerk gives a shoehorn and asked if the customer would like to try padded inserts or lifetime guarantee socks. (Sometimes add-ons are sold, sometimes given away.) A clerk at a supermarket hands customers a few candy kisses with the receipt—an unexpected thank-you. The paint store clerk checks to be sure the customer has caulking and sandpaper, which might have been forgotten.

One of my favorites: The drive-in teller at a bank has long given lollipops to kids in the car, but now offers a dog biscuit to customers with dogs in the car.

My son refuses to rent videos anywhere except the place that gave him a free bag of popcorn. I always fill the car's tank where I get a free car wash. The costs of these add-ons? I'm told the popcorn costs 4 cents and the car wash 7 cents. Those pennies buy a lot of customer loyalty.

What add-on product or service can you give *your* customers?

35.
E-Plus with convenience.

The fastest-growing businesses are those that offer added convenience. It wasn't too many years ago when getting the oil changed in your car meant leaving the vehicle all day at a service station. Today, lube centers will do the job in 15 minutes while you wait in a comfortable area.

Pizza would not likely be America's favorite food if it were not for quick home or office delivery. I visited a tie store that offered to deliver a tie to my office (in case I got razzed about the ugly one I wore or had an important meeting come up). This same store has a "tie of the month" promotion. They send customers a color photocopied sheet showing several of the newest offerings. The customer calls, and the tie is delivered.

Convenience is especially important when dealing with a product problem. The typical response to a customer with a faulty product is "bring it in and we'll replace it." That is *E* but not E-Plus. Toyota's Lexus division did it better when handling a recall. Dealers called customers for an appointment to pick up the car. They left a loaner car, and some dealers even left a rose or a $50 bill on the seat to apologize for the inconvenience! The outcome? Customers were exposed to the exceptional service department, and an embarrassment became what one Toyota executive called "a watershed event" for getting customers into the dealer's shop.

How can you make things more convenient for your customers?

36.
Identify and improve your POEs.

Make a list of each of your company's *points of encounter* (POEs) with customers or potential customers. Then focus your efforts on making these POEs smooth, professional and pleasant.

Your customer's POEs probably include the point at which he:

1. First hears about your business or becomes aware of what you do.

2. Makes contact with you either in person or by phone.

3. Waits to be served.

4. Is introduced to your products or services.

5. Tries out your product.

6. Experiences your follow-up.

7. Encounters the way you handle problems.

What potential problems might the customer face at each of these POEs? For the first POE, he may not be clear as to what you do, or may have concerns about your ability or willingness to help him. He may be impressed (favorably or negatively) with your organization's logo, slogans, work location or the like.

50 Ways to Win New Customers

For the second POE, the customer may be put off by appearances or mannerisms that project low professionalism or unfriendliness.

For the third POE, he may be frustrated by delays or the boredom of having to wait. (Walt Disney World spent a lot of effort developing ways to reduce the boredom of waiting in lines for rides. My local post office installed displays of interesting stamps and even a videotape player to keep its customers distracted.) Restaurants provide music or light reading. The Marriott hotel even posts the day's newspaper above the urinals in the men's room to keep us busy folks occupied!

The fourth and fifth POEs involve the people skills of your customer contact people. Getting people to try the product immediately has a very positive impact on selling and satisfying. Computer dealers who sit the prospect down and have him punch a few keys and car dealers who get him in for a test drive are making the most of these POEs.

The sixth and seventh POEs can do a great deal to create a loyal repeat customer.

Think about your customer's POEs. (There may be others in addition to these seven.) Then make these as smooth and professional as possible.

37.
Anticipate customer needs.

Helen, a middle-aged woman, was hired to work in a local department store during the Christmas season. During a particularly hectic day, a young, pregnant mother with two toddlers holding onto her approached Helen's cash register. Spotting the woman, Helen excused herself from the other customers for a moment and took a chair from behind the counter to the young woman.

"Why don't you sit down here," she asked, "and I'll ring up your purchases in a few minutes and bring them back to you."

The shopper was astounded and appreciative!

All Helen had done was *anticipate customer needs* and then did something about them. She won a loyal customer for that store through her initiative and good sense.

Other ways we might anticipate and meet needs:

- **Be sure the customer has everything needed** to use the product (If he buys paint, for example, ask if he has enough brushes, thinner, sandpaper, etc.)

- **Offer to carry merchandise** to the customer's car.

- **Respond to the customer's urgency.** If she's in a hurry, work quickly to accommodate.

50 Ways to Win New Customers

- **Help reduce confusion.** If an application form is difficult, show your customer which parts he needs to complete and you fill in the rest.

- **Be sure your customer has enough information** to use the product or service. (If written directions or clarification would be useful, write some and provide photocopies to customers.)

- **Make your work place barrier-free and easily accessible.** Open areas look better and allow easier communication.

- **Be available when your customers need you.** Years ago banks closed at 2 p.m. and most stores by 6. People today expect more. Car dealers are starting to have extended service department hours (some even 24 hours!) Government agencies have been notorious for being open when working people can't get there, but that, too, is improving.

- **Have large, clear signs** both inside and outside your business place.

38.
Help your customers feel at home.

A small college bookstore in rural Ohio was featured in a story in *The Wall Street Journal* because it offered a special homey feeling. It offered something the large discount chains cannot: a second living room.

The story reports that "here customers can sit in armchairs, eat Ben & Jerry's ice cream and read all day without buying a thing. They can even leaf through magazines, make a copy of an article and put the publication back on the shelf—without getting a cold stare from an employee."[6]

Does this make good business sense? The store manager thinks so. He believes that customers buy more when there is no pressure to buy. "The more we seem to try *not* to sell things, the more we sell," he says. He attributes the low-pressure approach to helping him quadruple sales over the past 10 years.

The store also became a place where students and faculty members could relax and chat over a cup of coffee. In short, this store tries to make people feel at home.

---

[6] "College Bookstore Invites Its Customers to Curl Up," *The Wall Street Journal*, August 27, 1992, p. B2.

39.
Consider the possibility of doing away with salespeople.

Buying an automobile has long been a stressful experience for people. It's a large-ticket item and customers often feel they are getting skinned, especially if they are not skilled negotiators.

Saturn Division of General Motors was one of the first to go to fixed pricing on cars. The sticker price is actually what the car costs. (A revolutionary idea!?) But because the price is not negotiated, customers deal with product information specialists—not salespeople. The customer knows what it'll cost, the employee teaches about the features and benefits of the product.

Ford has applied a similar policy to the sale of its Escort cars and many individual dealers are going to fixed pricing. In many cases, salespeople are taken off commission and paid a fixed salary. The company's culture changes and customers feel more comfortable.

40.
Listen with more than your ears.

There is no such thing as an unpopular listener. Almost everyone becomes more interesting when he stops talking. Pay attention to your talk-listen ratio. Are you giving the customer equal time or better?

To be a better listener, use these ideas:

- **Judge the content** of what people are saying, *not the way they are saying it*. Customers may not have the "right" words, but they know what they need better than anyone.

- **Hold your fire.** Don't jump to make judgments before your customer has finished talking.

- **Work at listening.** Maintain eye contact and discipline yourself to listen to what is being said. Tune out those thoughts that get you thinking about something else.

- **Resist distractions.** Make the customer the center of your attention.

- **Seek clarification** from customers so you fully understand their needs. Do this in a non-threatening way using sincere, open-ended questions.

41.
Make your office customer-friendly.

Be sensitive to layout and decor. Check for barriers. Often people arrange their workspace so that there is a desk or table between them and the customer. While sometimes this is necessary, often it creates an unnecessary barrier. Try inviting customers to sit beside your desk with you instead of across from you. Try using a small round table, especially when customers need to read materials you give them.

Some auto dealerships removed all sales office desks and replaced them with small round tables. Now the customer and salesperson sit around the table and work *together* to make a deal.

Finally, look for customer comfort. Are your customers invited to sit in a comfortable chair? Does your office or store invite them to relax? Are waiting areas furnished with reading materials, perhaps a TV? Are vending machines available? Is the vending area kept clean?

A small auto body shop I visited surprised me. It had a waiting room that looked like a living room. Easy chairs, a TV, coffee table with magazines, even fresh flowers. Take a look at your work areas from the customer's viewpoint.

Incidentally, I heard of an interesting layout idea used by the manager who handled the more serious complaints at a business. He mounted a large mirror behind his desk so that irate complainers had to see themselves as he saw them. This cooled off a lot of people!

42.
Develop verbal discipline.

Train your self-talk and your comments to others to focus on the positive, and avoid being judgmental. Instead of stereotyping people into some negative category and labeling them with a derogatory term, look for neutral or positive words. Instead of saying, "This guy will nickel and dime me to death," say "This customer is cost-conscious."

At times you'll have to force yourself to avoid the negative and judgmental, but accept the challenge and you can make a game out of it.

Sincerely try for one full day to avoid saying anything negative or judgmental about another person. If you make it through the day, shoot for another day. Verbal discipline can become a habit that pays off.

You'll find yourself enjoying people more.

43.
Use good telephone techniques.

Often your only contact with customers is via the phone. Make the most of it.

A key to successful phone use is to simply *remember that your customer cannot see you.* Your challenge is to make up for all that lost nonverbal communication by using your voice effectively.

The best ways to use the phone effectively:

- **Give the caller your name.** Let the caller know who you are just as you would in a face-to-face situation (via a name tag or desk plaque).

- **Smile into the phone.** Somehow people can hear a smile over the phone! Some telephone pros place a mirror in front of them while they're on the phone.

- **Keep your caller informed.** If you need to look up information, tell the customer what you are doing. Don't leave them holding a dead phone with no clue as to whether you are still with him or her.

- **Invite the caller to get to the point.** Use questions such as "How can I assist you today?" or "What can I do for you?"

- **Commit to requests of the caller.** Tell the caller specifically what you will do and when you will get back to him or her. ("I'll check on this billing problem and get back to you by 5 this afternoon, OK?")

- **Thank the caller.** This lets the caller know when the conversation is over.

- **Let your voice fluctuate in tone, rate and loudness.** You hold people's attention by putting a little life into your voice. Express honest reactions in expressive ways. Let your voice tones be natural and friendly.

- **Use hold carefully.** People hate being put on hold. When it's necessary, explain why and break in periodically to let your caller know he or she hasn't been forgotten. If what you're doing will take longer than a few minutes, ask the caller if you can call him or her back. *Write down your commitment to call back and don't miss it!*

- **Use friendly, tactful words.** Never accuse the customer of anything; never convey that his or her request is an imposition.

Part 5
Networking

44.
Ask for referrals.

Always ask a satisfied customer for the names of people who might also like to buy from you. Get addresses and phone numbers and follow through with a call or a card.

While this is a common practice in some industries, it can also be used in hundreds of other situations. Call referred people to introduce yourself and invite them to come to your business. Most people will be surprised and pleased by a personal invitation like that. And it beats sitting around hoping someone will come in.

Of course, the more information you can get about a referred person the better. But don't make referral-giving a big job for your customer. A name and address or phone number is all you need. You can look up other data if necessary.

Bill, my friend in the insurance business, says this when he has closed a customer: "There are two ways you can pay me in this business. First, I need the names of people you know who could benefit from what I just sold you. Second, I need a check from you." In phrasing it this way, Bill placed heavy importance on the value of the referral. Even before he got the customer's money, he asked for referrals!

Referrals can be that valuable.

45.
Remember
Girard's Law of 250.

Sales trainer Joe Girard claims that everyone knows about 250 people. Where does he come up with that number? He figures that's about how many people are likely to show up for a typical funeral or wedding.[7]

I don't suggest you start pestering everyone you remotely know to buy your stuff; it probably isn't right for everyone. But starting a prospect list with who you know is always productive.

But, beware! While the 250 acquaintances your customers know may be a great source for you to tap, if you give poor customer service, word will filter out to the 250 people your customer knows and you'll find yourself playing catch-up. As Girard illustrates:

> *"If I see 50 people in a week, and only two of them are unhappy with the way I treat them, at the end of the year there will be 5,000 people influenced by just those two a week. I've been selling cars for 14 years. So if I turned off just two people a week out of all that*

---

[7] Joe actually came up with this number by asking funeral directors how many mass cards (with the name and picture of the departed) they typically printed. Funeral directors said "about 250" come to pay last respects to the deceased. Weddings are another indicator of the typical person's circle of friends and acquaintances. Again, the number comes out to about 250 for each person. Obviously some people know fewer but many know more, and the 250 seems a good average figure.

50 Ways to Win New Customers

I see, there would be 70,000 people, a whole stadium full, who know one thing for sure: Don't buy a car from Joe Girard!"[8]

Remember the devastating cost of bad ripple effects. But also remember that the ripples flow both ways. Happy customers will tell their network of friends about E-Plus service, too.

Multilevel or network marketing uses this to maximum advantage by giving customers commissions on sales they have influenced. This can get pretty complicated, but here is a simple application:

A barber in Detroit has a sign on the wall. It says, "Ask me to explain how you can make $25." When asked, the barber tells his customers that if they refer a friend to a particular car dealer, and the referral eventually buys a car, the dealer will pay them $25. He then gives the customer 10 of the dealer's business cards and puts his or her name and phone number on the back. The barber gets $1 for every card he gives out. This dealer outsold every other dealership in the United States, several years running.[9]

Does $1 a card seem too high? Maybe not if you are selling $20,000 cars. But the point of the story is that this business was using the principle of networking. Perhaps the barber would do the same task in exchange for free oil changes and minor service on his car.

Make it a practice to look for ways you can network with other people.

---

[8] Joe Girard, *How to Sell Anything to Anybody* (New York: Simon and Schuster, 1977), p. 48.

[9] This story was told in Gallagher, Wilson, and Levinson's book *Guerrilla Selling* (Houghton Mifflin, 1993), pp. 30-31.

Part 6
Restoration of the lost customer

46.
Listen to the customers you *didn't* get.

When people indicate that they bought from a competitor, ask why. Not in an argumentative way, but with sincerity. Simply say that you would have liked to gain their business and ask why they chose another company.

Listen carefully to what they say and you'll get some good tips on how to improve your business.

In every business we can learn from mistakes. It takes courage (and often a thick skin) to ask people what you did wrong. But it can be some of the most useful information you'll ever get.

Remember, the ostrich leaves one end exposed.

47.
Don't write off the goofed customer.

OK, so you messed up with customers in the past. They bought something that didn't work or one of your people gave them a hard time. Is all lost? Nope.

It's funny, but true: Customers who have a problem with a company—and the company works hard to fix the problem—actually become more loyal than customers who have never had a problem. Apparently companies and people who develop their "recovery" skills end up with more loyal customers.

Recognize that upset customers want some or all of the following from you:

- To be listened to and taken seriously.
- That you understand their problem and the reason they are upset.
- Compensation or restitution.
- A sense of urgency; to get their problem handled quickly.
- Avoidance of further inconvenience.
- To be treated with respect.
- To have someone punished for the problem.
- Assurance that the problem will not occur again.

If all goes well, you should feel a genuine sense of satisfaction after handling an unhappy or irate customer. But this is not a perfect world and people are not always rational, so sometimes you, too, get upset. The key things to remember are:

- **If you try your best to satisfy** the customer, you have done all that you can do.
- **Don't take it personally.** Upset people often say things they don't really mean. They are blowing off steam, venting frustration. If the problem was really your fault, resolve to learn from the experience and do better next time. If you had no control over the situation, do what you can, but don't bat your head against the wall.
- **Don't rehash the experience** with your co-workers or in your own mind. What's done is done. Recounting the experience with others probably won't make their day any better, and rehashing it to yourself will just make you mad. You may, however, want to ask another person how they would have handled the situation.
- Use every customer contact experience as an **opportunity to improve**. Even the most unpleasant encounter can teach us useful lessons.

When the situation has cooled, you may want to review with an eye toward improving your skills. Think back on the situation where you used your recovery skills and ask questions like these:

- What was the customer's major complaint?
- How did the customer see the problem? Who was to blame? What irritated the customer most? Why was he or she angry/frustrated?

- How did you see the problem? Was the customer partially to blame?

- What did you say to the customer that helped the situation?

- What did you say that seemed to aggravate the situation?

- How did you try to show your concern to the customer?

- What would you do differently?

48.
Apologize.

Some people hate to apologize on behalf of the company, especially when the problem was not one they had direct control over.

Apologizing does not diminish you. It does not need to be an admission of guilt. An apology is an expression of regret that the customer's experience has been less than pleasant.

Giving an apology takes nothing away from you! It expresses the wish that future customer experiences will be more positive. But without an apology, there will be no future customer experiences.

49.
Tell how you fixed it.

Part of customer relations is public relations and the first rule of public relations is to *let good deeds be noticed*. If a customer has a problem and you fix it, tell that customer, and, in some cases, tell other customers, too.

Follow-up calls to repair customers to be sure that their problem has been solved (even if you know it has been) reminds them that you care.

Example: An auto service department replaced my car's radio immediately rather than removing it and sending it off for repair. The service manager said he didn't want me to be "driving around with a hole in my dashboard" like other dealers might have me do. A reminder that he'd given me E-Plus service.

A bookstore owner called several competitors to see if they had a title I was looking for. Then he called me back to say what he'd done and where I could find it.

50.
Ask the magic question, "What can I do to make it right?

You can quote me. Go ahead, use the exact words. But ask this question often and sincerely.

The question invites customer participation in solving the problem. It reflects concern, interest in solving the problem, and respect for the customer's wishes.

Try it.

A final
few words

50 Ways to Win New Customers

So there you have them. Fifty ways to win new customers. Are there others? Of course. There are as many ways as there are customers and products. Anyone can come up with new ideas like these. They're everywhere!

I hope this book stimulates you to sharpen your attitude of inquiry. It really is an attitude, you know. Some people experience thousands of business transactions and never even see what made them work or fail in winning customers. Other people tune in to the process and generate countless ideas they can apply immediately. The determining factor is their attitude of inquiry.

Keep your eyes open. Recognize clever and interesting approaches used by businesses to entice you to buy. Then see which of these might apply to your line of work. You may be surprised at the frequency with which an application can be made.

Getting customers is an art and a science. An art because it calls for creativity and innovation; a science because it call for systematic application of ideas and examination of the results.

Make it your goal—starting today—to apply the customer-getting ideas described in this book as well as others they may trigger in your mind. Try on some new behaviors and carefully observe the results. You'll be pleasantly surprised at your success in winning new customers.

> *"Whoever acquires knowledge but*
> *does not practice it, is as one who*
> *ploughs but does not sow."*
> —Saadi

About the author

Dr. Paul R. Timm has written 18 books and scores of articles in the fields of customer service, human relations, communication and self-management. He holds a doctorate degree from Florida State University in organizational communication and is Chair of the Department of Management Communication in the Marriott School of Management at Brigham Young University.

As an active consultant and trainer, Timm has worked with thousands of people from organizations throughout North America. He wrote and appears in three videotape training programs sold worldwide including *The Power of Customer Service, Successful Self-Management,* and *50 Ways to Keep Your Customers* (available through JWA Televideo, Chicago. Call (312) 829-5100 to order.) He is the author of *50 Powerful Ideas You Can Use To Keep Your Customers* (available through Career Press. Call 1-800-CAREER-1 to order.)

For information about Timm's consulting and training services, including the powerful *More Customers* executive workshops, call 801-378-5682.

Index

50 Ways to Win New Customers

50 Ways to Win New Customers